A VIEW from the RIVER

THE CHICAGO ARCHITECTURE FOUNDATION RIVER CRUISE

CHICAGO ARCHITECTURE FOUNDATION

Text by Jennifer Marjorie Bosch

Photographs by Hedrich Blessing

Pomegranate

SAN FRANCISCO

Published by Pomegranate Communications, Inc.

Box 808022, Petaluma, CA 94975

800 227 1428 www.pomegranate.com

Pomegranate Europe Ltd.

Unit 1, Heathcote Business Centre, Hurlbutt Road

Warwick, Warwickshire CV34 6TD

United Kingdom

[+44] 0 1926 430111 sales@pomeurope.co.uk

Library of Congress Cataloging-in-Publication Data

Bosch, Jennifer Marjorie.

   A view from the river : the Chicago Architecture Foundation river cruise / text by Jennifer Marjorie Bosch ; photographs by Hedrich Blessing.

      p. cm.

   Includes index.

   ISBN-13: 978-0-7649-4532-8

1. Architecture–Illinois–Chicago–Guidebooks. 2. Chicago (Ill.)–Buildings, structures, etc.–Guidebooks. 3. Chicago (Ill.)–Guidebooks. 4. Chicago River (Ill.)–Guidebooks. I. Title: Chicago Architecture Foundation river cruise. II. Hedrich-Blessing (Firm) III. Chicago Architecture Foundation. IV. Title.

   NA735.C4P75 2008

   720.9773'11–dc22

                                    2007051449

Pomegranate Catalog No. A148

ISBN 978-0-7649-4532-8

Design by Monroe Street Studios, Santa Rosa, California

Printed in Korea

17 16 15 14 13 12 11 10 09   10 9 8 7 6 5 4 3 2

CONTENTS

CHICAGO ARCHITECTURE FOUNDATION

the Chicago Architecture Foundation engages audiences in exploring Chicago's architectural legacy. Since 1966 the organization has advanced public interest and education in the built environment through tours, exhibitions, and youth and adult programs. Serving as a forum for dialogue about architecture, infrastructure, and design, the Chicago Architecture Foundation promotes sustainable communities for the twenty-first century.

Chicago Architecture Foundation
224 South Michigan Avenue
Chicago IL 60604
312.922.3432
www.architecture.org

FOREWORD

explosive growth during the second half of the nineteenth century brought Chicago international renown as an industrial powerhouse. Today Chicago is completing its transition from manufacturing and commerce to a service- and recreation-based economy. Exploring the Chicago River, which has played a central role in the city's history, is an ideal way to learn how Chicago and all other cities change.

After fire leveled much of the metropolis in 1871, the architects, engineers, and industrialists who converged here created masterpieces of design. The work of legendary Chicago-based architects such as Louis Sullivan, Daniel Burnham, and Frank Lloyd Wright inspired architects around the world. Community activists and social science innovators like Jane Addams and Robert E. Park used Chicago as a laboratory as they pioneered new ways of understanding urban centers and city dwellers.

Chicago defined what it means to be modern. The World's Columbian Exposition of 1893 drew millions of visitors who witnessed both the dangers of city life and the potential of urban planning. Burnham and Bennett's 1909 *Plan of Chicago* presented a blueprint for how cities might be organized. Today Chicago's historic landscapes inspire the city as it transforms itself into a postindustrial community.

At the threshold of the twenty-first century, the global community must transform its attitudes toward the environment. Within fifty years, 75 percent of the world's population will live in urban environments; addressing this shift in density is critical to our survival and well-being. There are many challenges ahead—in housing, infrastructure, and sustainability.

The Chicago Architecture Foundation, founded in 1966, is a model for architecture centers worldwide. CAF's mission is to advance public interest and education in architecture and infrastructure. The organization offers a comprehensive range of activities including tours, exhibitions, lectures, special events, and youth and adult education programs. CAF inspires and challenges public audiences to understand how architects, engineers, and planners shape their lives—and how everyone can participate.

Chicago is the ideal place to experience architecture and infrastructure. And the Chicago Architecture Foundation River Cruise, on the Chicago's First Lady fleet, provides a perfect vantage point for learning about the design of our environment and thinking about its future.

Lynn J. Osmond, President, Chicago Architecture Foundation

DOCENT ACKNOWLEDGMENTS

*I*n 1983 the Chicago Architecture Foundation's first River Cruise was developed by Robert F. Irving, a member of the first docent class of 1971. Since then the tour has attracted over 175,000 people annually, making it one of the most popular tourist attractions in Chicago. CAF is grateful to the one hundred volunteer river docents who are dedicated to giving quality tours for visitors, rain or shine.

River Cruise Docents 2007

Helene Albert	Karen Dimond	Bennett Johnson	David Pierson
Tom Allabastro	Rebecca Dixon	Gina Johnson	Bobbi Pinkert
James Allan	Syma Dodson	Tosh Junior	Tom Reynolds
Mary Allan	Sylvia Dunbeck	Eric Kille	Marcia Ross
Cindy Anderson	Linda Ewing	Tom Kinsella	Maureen Sauvé
Doug Anderson	Joan Fallert	Mili Kirsh	Pauline Scharres
Jurgis Anysas	Dan Fitzgerald	Art Kruski	Sydney Schuler
Diane Atwood	Matthew Fitzsimmons	Bill Lee	Polly Sippy
Geoffrey Baer	Karen Flannery	Peg Leonard	David Smith
Charles Berg	Debra Jean Frels	Alan Lessack	Ronnie Jo Sokol
Mari-Pat Boughner	Wayne Galasek	Jill Lowe	Chuck Solomonson
Sandy Bredine	Karen Genelly	Karen Luckritz	Hy Speck
Tom Burke	Steven Gersten	Mary Ludgin	Marie Spicuzza
Barbara Butz	Linda Goggin	Aileen Mandel	Charles Stanford
Jane Cahill	Patricia Grund	Mike McMains	Bronwein Stevens
Ron Campbell	Sandy Guettler	Hartley Meyer	Diane Stone
Deborah Carey	Cindy Hancock	Bill Myers	Toni Substalae
Athene Carras	Joy Hebert	Jonelle Niffenegger	Lindy Trigg
John Chaput	Judy Hennig	Anita North-Hamill	Adina Van Buren
Patricia Lee Cody	Margaret Hicks	Nancy Nusser	Mitzi Walchak
Henry Cohen	Bill Hinchliff	Susan Osborn	Donald Wiberg
Nancy Cook	Harry Hirsch	Susan Pappas	Joyce Wiberg
Marcia Wachs Dam	Bob Irving	Gail Peace	Nancy Loewenberg Young
Carlos de la Fuente	Marshall Jacobson	Don Peterson	Frank Youngwerth
Matthew Defty	Jim Javorcic	Tom Phillips	

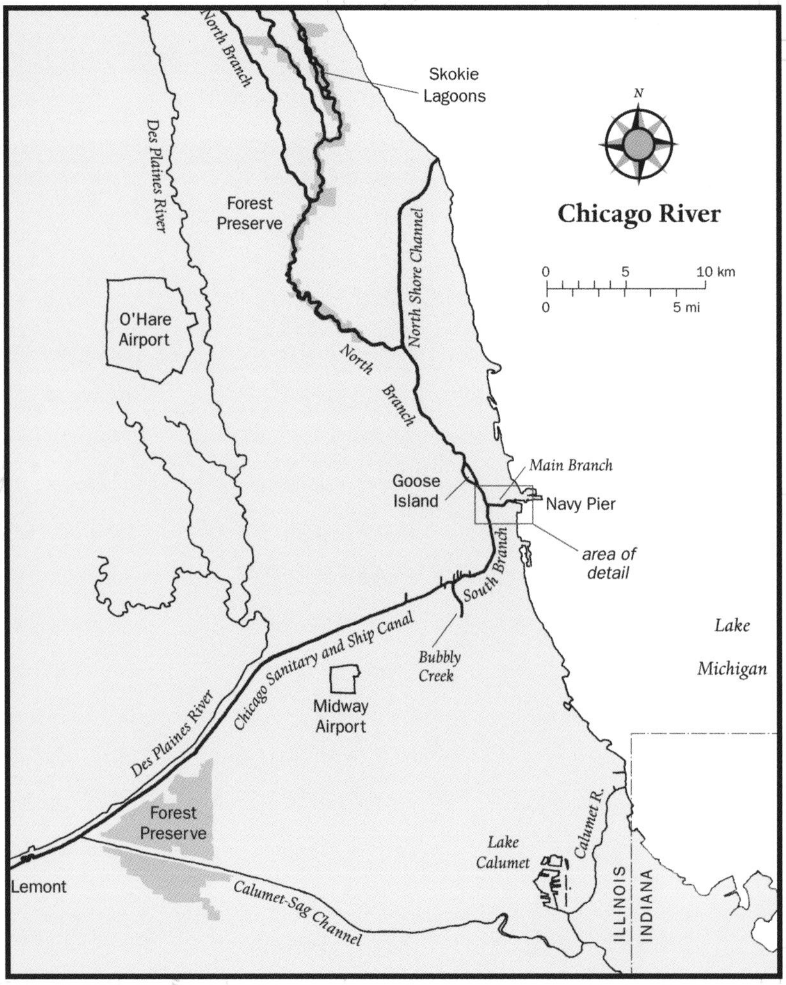

Chicago River

Skokie Lagoons

North Branch

Des Plaines River

Forest Preserve

North Shore Channel

O'Hare Airport

North Branch

Goose Island

Main Branch

Navy Pier

area of detail

South Branch

Chicago Sanitary and Ship Canal

Bubbly Creek

Midway Airport

Des Plaines River

Lake Michigan

Forest Preserve

Lake Calumet

Calumet R.

ILLINOIS
INDIANA

Lemont

Calumet-Sag Channel

N

0   5   10 km

0   5 mi

Image courtesy of Friends of the Chicago River

INTRODUCTION

The buildings that rise along the banks of the Chicago River tell stories of the city's growth, its architectural legacy, and the use and restoration of its waterways. To understand these stories is to understand the link between city, buildings, and river.

The Chicago River consists of three parts. The Main Branch runs west from Lake Michigan through downtown. The North Branch originates almost at the Wisconsin border and flows south to Wolf Point, at the west end of the Main Branch. From there, the South Branch flows south into the Sanitary and Ship Canal. This book is divided into branches. It follows the route of the Chicago Architecture Foundation's River Cruise.

Chicago's harbor, 1831

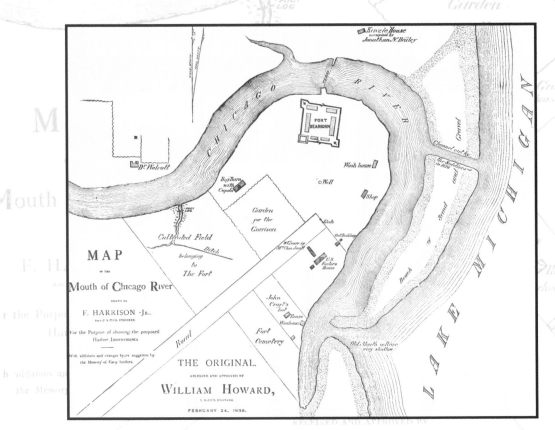

The mouth of the Chicago River, 1830

THE MAIN BRANCH

*f*our hundred years ago, the Chicago River and Lake Michigan facilitated travel and trade among Native Americans. In the mid-seventeenth century, French fur traders made their living from the waterways, the surrounding prairies, and the woods. When Father Jacques Marquette and Louis Jolliet explored the region in 1674, they recognized the river's potential to help connect the Atlantic Ocean, the Great Lakes, and the Gulf of Mexico.

Settlers who arrived in the 1830s beheld a waterway vastly different from today's. Some called it a stream; it was slow-moving, marshy, and emptied into Lake Michigan approximately one-half mile south of where it now empties. A sandbar blocked direct access to the river and made entry dangerous for boats. But builders transformed the river, lining it with timber retaining walls, docks, wharves, turnarounds, grain elevators, and warehouses. The river became a symbol of the burgeoning city's agricultural, commercial, and industrial strength. It also became Chicago's sewer.

The rise of railroads, the growth of Chicago as a business center, the 1909 *Plan of Chicago,* the extension of Michigan Avenue across the river in 1920, improved sewage treatment and storm-water control, the establishment of the Environmental Protection Agency in 1970, the rise of the postindustrial economy—these were all factors in the transformations of the Chicago River.

Chicago's harbor today

The Lake Locks Offer a Lesson in Infrastructure

Settlers built Chicago on swampy land. They dug pit toilets and shallow wells; they dumped animal waste into the streets. When it rained, every hole and depression—including the wells from which drinking water was drawn—became a pool of mud and sewage. Ditches running to the river helped drain water and waste, but the ditches became clogged.

Because of typhus and cholera outbreaks, the city raised the entire street grade in the late 1850s to construct a sewer system that emptied directly into the river. The resulting pollution threatened the city's main source of potable water, an intake crib in Lake Michigan. To protect the lake and bring clean water into the river, engineers reversed the river's flow in 1900 and connected it to the Des Plaines River southwest of the city via a 28-mile canal. The canal was deeper than the river, which at its mouth was deeper than Lake Michigan. Gravity pulled clean water from the lake into the river and then into the canal—and away from the city.

At first the city did not regulate the quantity of water drawn from Lake Michigan. But nearby Great Lakes states put legal pressure on Chicago to limit diverted water. In 1930 the federal government forced Chicago to build a lock at the river's mouth, limiting lake water intake to about two billion gallons per day.

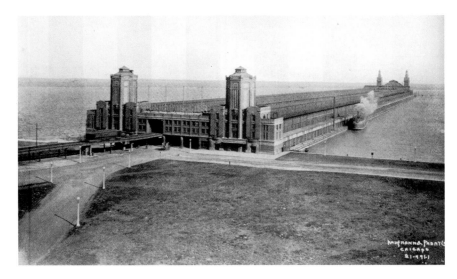

Navy Pier, circa 1929

Navy Pier

Charles S. Frost: original design, 1916

Jerome R. Butler Jr.: restoration of east auditorium building, 1976

Benjamin Thompson & Associates; VOA Associates: major pier renovation, 1995

In his 1909 *Plan of Chicago,* Daniel Burnham proposed a modernized harbor facility with two recreational piers; only one pier was realized, north of the Main Branch. The structure, originally called Municipal Pier, included a cargo facility, warehouses, an auditorium, a streetcar line, a restaurant, and grand views of Lake Michigan. During World War I, the pier housed Red Cross and home defense offices, carrier pigeon stations, and a jail for draft dodgers. After the war, the pier's name was changed to honor veterans. Navy Pier's popularity peaked in the 1920s, but the Great Depression and new leisure options—like drive-ins and amusement parks—sped its decline as a public attraction in the 1930s. The navy leased the pier during World War II and trained more than 60,000 troops on site. To educate returning veterans, the University of Illinois converted the pier to a campus.

In the 1970s Navy Pier's future was uncertain. A $200 million renovation in the 1990s added restaurants, a ballroom, stages, exhibition halls, IMAX and Shakespeare theaters, a Ferris wheel, and museums dedicated to stained glass and to children.

Lake Point Tower

Schipporeit-Heinrich; Graham, Anderson, Probst & White, 1968

Just west of the pier, Lake Point Tower demands attention. Schipporeit-Heinrich apparently based the building's design on a 1921 sketch made by Ludwig Mies van der Rohe—their former teacher and employer. Instead of the four wings called for in Mies's design, the architects gave the structure a Y shape in order to provide better views and ventilation, while reducing the impact of the wind.

At the time of construction, Lake Point Tower's location was controversial. In 1836 Chicago's founding fathers had decreed that the city's lakefront was to be "public ground—a common to remain forever open, clear, and free of any buildings, or other obstruction whatever." This dictum was not strictly observed. In 1964 the city planning department reaffirmed the need to protect the lakefront from development, with the exception of land on both sides of the river's mouth—most of which was owned by Chicago Dock and Canal Trust. The exception was meant to encourage improved harbor and terminal facilities rather than residential development. But that same year the trust leased its land to a Texas-based company that began to erect a skyscraper. Subsequently the planning commission closed the loophole with an amendment that banned multistory buildings from the water's edge. But it was too late to halt construction of Lake Point Tower.

Lakeshore East

(left) The Chandler
   DeStefano & Partners; Loewenberg Architects, 2007

(rear center) The Lancaster
   Skidmore, Owings & Merrill; Loewenberg Architects, 2005

(center) The Regatta
   DeStefano & Partners; Loewenberg Architects, 2007

(right of center) The Shoreham
   Loewenberg Architects, 2005

(right) 340 on the Park
   Solomon Cordwell Buenz, 2007

Looking at Lakeshore East's numerous construction projects, one can hardly imagine this location as a former landfill. The development's motto—"Where the river meets the lake"—would not have been a selling point for a residential community in the early 1900s, given the condition of the river. Today many buildings celebrate their proximity to the water in design and concept. Residences such as the Regatta and the Shoreham feature tinted glass, curving balconies, and green spaces meant to harmonize with the Chicago River and Lake Michigan. Such touches distinguish the Lakeshore East buildings from the modernist skyscrapers of the Illinois Center, built immediately to the west.

Blue Cross Blue Shield Building

Lohan Associates, 1997

When architect James Goettsch began work on the Blue Cross Blue Shield Building, he focused on his client's requirements. BCBS had asked for a building that would promote interdepartmental communication and could expand with the company's anticipated growth—by as much as 800,000 square feet over the next sixteen years. Goettsch's design met those demands and more. He incorporated atrium stairways that allow employees to travel easily between departments, to confer quickly on the landings, and to get a little extra exercise. The atrium extends the full height of the building, offering natural light and space for additional elevators. The foundation and structural system of the thirty-two-story structure were designed to accommodate the addition of twenty-five more stories. The expansion is slated for completion in 2010.

The future Illinois Center property, circa 1929

Illinois Center

(center) Three Illinois Center, Office of Mies van der Rohe, 1979

One of Chicago's most extensive real estate developments occupies land that was once the rail yard of the Illinois Central (IC). Today this area is called the Illinois Center; it is bordered by Randolph Street, Michigan Avenue, the Chicago River, and Lake Shore Drive.

In the 1840s Lake Michigan bordered Michigan Avenue. Though city founders had demanded that the lakeshore remain forever clear and free, the federal government allowed the IC to build a trestle in the water (at modern-day Columbus Drive) that linked railroad lines to the busy port. After the Great Fire of 1871, the city filled the land between Michigan Avenue and the trestle with debris. The southern portion of the debris field became Grant Park; the IC turned the northern portion into its terminus and freight yard.

The twentieth century brought a decline in river traffic, and IC officials wanted to sell their air rights (that is, permission to build above the tracks) for development. As early as the 1920s, there were plans to build a business district over the tracks, but the Great Depression and World War II halted progress. The city and the IC battled over ownership of air rights for decades, until in 1966 the courts ruled in favor of the IC. Shortly thereafter the railroad company began working with the Office of Mies van der Rohe to develop a 30-year plan for an 83-acre, multiuse, trilevel city-within-a-city. The first of the development's buildings to be completed was One Illinois Center, which opened in 1971.

Aon Center

(far left) Edward Durrell Stone; Perkins & Will, 1973

The Aon Center is sometimes called "the building that was built twice." When first erected, the structure was sheathed in Italian Carrara marble—the same kind used by Michelangelo. Its 43,000 panels, however, could not handle Chicago's temperature fluctuations, and they began to buckle. The owners replaced the marble with North Carolina granite at a cost of about $80 million, more than half of the original construction cost of $120 million. The scrapped marble—all 6,000 tons of it—had a second life as trinkets, trophies, and landscaping stone.

Swissôtel Chicago

(far right) Harry Weese & Associates, 1989

Architect Harry Weese loved boats, so it is not surprising to find several of his buildings along the river. The design of the Swissôtel reflects the architect's passion. The building is triangular, reminiscent of a sail. The shape offers unobstructed views of the river and the lake.

2 Prudential Plaza

(rear center) Loebl, Schlossman & Hackl, 1990

Between the Aon Center and the Swissôtel rises the chevron-shaped pinnacle of "2 Pru," 2 Prudential Plaza. During the design process, architect Steve Wright of Loebl, Schlossman & Hackl created its signature peak. "To do all that work and then just plop a cooling tower or electronic switching box on the roof seems unfortunate. . . . I wanted the top to be an integral part of the design." Wright designed a beveled art deco pyramid top with a 40-foot stainless-steel spire. This glittering peak hides the building's four water cooling tanks. The open spaces in the bevels aid the cooling process.

CITYFRONT CENTER—
From Shacks to Skyscrapers

Chicago's first mayor, William B. Ogden, had a thriving lumber business. As an investment and a means of expediting the shipment of his lumber, Ogden began to acquire most of the land within an area today bordered by Michigan Avenue, Chicago Avenue, Lake Michigan, and the river. He took over lake frontage by burning down the shacks and brothels on the land he coveted. In order to acquire properties he could not purchase outright, Ogden formed the Dock and Canal Company, whose stated mission was to benefit the public through development of the north riverbank. The true beneficiary, of course, was Ogden.

Except for the construction of warehouses and grain elevators, no development took place on this parcel of land for most of the twentieth century because there was no direct street access. It was not until the 1982 completion of the Columbus Drive Bridge that the area became easily accessible. Subsequently the renamed Chicago Dock and Canal Trust joined the Equitable Life Assurance Society of the United States to launch a major planned development, Cityfront Center.

The trust took charge of the land east of Columbus Drive, and Equitable handled the western portion. With the help of Chicago architects such as Skidmore, Owings & Merrill and Lohan Associates, the developers established zoning ordinances that provided public access to the riverfront, limited density and height, and preserved large green spaces—in contrast to the Illinois Center just across the river.

RiverView Condominiums and Townhouses

DeStefano & Partners, 2001

RiverView consists of two high-rise towers that sit atop a base of four-story townhouses. Its porthole windows, brick and limestone cladding, and green trim pay homage to its waterfront location and the warehouses that once stood on the site.

Nicholas J. Melas Centennial Fountain

Lohan Associates, 1989

Centennial Fountain honors the one-hundredth anniversary of the Metropolitan Water Reclamation District of Greater Chicago (formerly known as the Sanitary District). Architect Dirk Lohan, a grandson of Ludwig Mies van der Rohe, designed a fountain that represents the continental divide located just southwest of Chicago.

Prior to 1900 the river used to flow into the lake, the source of Chicago's drinking water. But the river was so polluted that it threatened the city's water supply. In order to send polluted water away from the lake, the Sanitary District reversed the flow of the Chicago River.

Today the Metropolitan Water Reclamation District is constructing more than 130 miles of underground tunnels and reservoirs. This project is the Tunnel and Reservoir Plan, nicknamed the "Deep Tunnel." Because Chicago has a combined sewer system (storm water and sewage drain into the same pipes), heavy rains can cause raw sewage to flow into the river, Lake Michigan, and local basements. In the 1970s this happened on an average of every four days. Since sections of the Deep Tunnel system began to operate in 2006, excess storm water and sewage have been diverted to reservoirs until treatment plants can process them.

Equitable Building

(center) Skidmore, Owings & Merrill, 1965

The Equitable Building is clad in bronze-tinted aluminum with bronze-toned windows and black spandrels. The prior landowner, the Tribune Company, agreed to sell only if the new building featured a riverfront walkway. This was prescient: it was not until 1998 that the city required all new waterside buildings to provide access to the river.

University of Chicago Gleacher Center

(center, low) Lohan Associates, 1994

Situated between NBC Tower and the Equitable Building, the Gleacher Center houses the University of Chicago's Graham School of General Studies and the part-time programs of the Graduate School of Business. This building has created a downtown identity distinct from the Hyde Park campus on the city's South Side. Its design evokes several architectural styles. The masonry facade reflects the main campus's Gothic Revival buildings. The glass and steel acknowledge the modernism of Ludwig Mies van der Rohe, architect Dirk Lohan's grandfather. The glass walls on the north and south ends enclose student lounges.

NBC Tower

(right) Skidmore, Owings & Merrill, 1989

Since the 1830s city officials had regulated fireproofing and building heights. But there had not been a city-wide zoning ordinance to address design. At the turn of the century, the growing number of skyscrapers raised concerns that streets would become dark canyons. In 1923 Chicago's first zoning ordinance was established. Buildings were permitted to occupy their full lot footprint up to a height of 264 feet. Above that, a tower could be added to a height of 600 feet. A tower's footprint could not take up more than 25 percent of the main building's footprint.

The postmodern design of NBC Tower acknowledges both the 1923 zoning ordinance and the neighboring Tribune Tower. Its first setback is at 264 feet, to mark the height of historic buildings along the river. Its second setback, at the twentieth floor, mirrors the setback of the Tribune Tower to the west.

The southeast tower of the Michigan Avenue Bridge

A Grand Gateway and Its Four Towers

At the turn of the century, businesses did not invest in the development of the north side of the river. Bridges were unreliable, and the city's priority was to keep the river unobstructed for the passage of ships. Warehouses, grain silos, lumber yards, and rail yards lined the riverbanks.

In the 1909 *Plan of Chicago,* Daniel Burnham envisioned extending Michigan Avenue across the river with a grand bridge. The hope was not only to provide access to the north but also to encourage construction of great architecture, similar to what was already found on the south side of the river. To demonstrate that Chicago was a city of culture and refinement, Edward Bennett designed a Beaux-Arts bascule bridge in 1917. Sculptural reliefs on each bridge tower record important moments in Chicago's history: the arrival of Marquette and Jolliet, early settlement, the Fort Dearborn massacre, and recovery from the Great Fire. This elegant gateway represented the faith that investors and businesses had in Chicago's future growth and improvement. Today the area north of the bridge is known as the Magnificent Mile.

Wrigley Building,
circa 1929

Wrigley Building

Graham, Anderson, Probst & White, 1921/1924

With the Michigan Avenue Bridge under construction, William Wrigley joined the efforts to expand Chicago's downtown business district north of the river. He hired one of the nation's most prestigious firms to design a glittering monument to Chicago—and to chewing gum.

In response to the property's challenging trapezoidal shape, architect Charles G. Beersman erected two buildings linked by a sky bridge. The Wrigley Building was clad in six shades of terra cotta—from light gray to pale cream to stark white—accenting the skyscraper's impressive height. When completed, it was Chicago's tallest building. For a quarter, visitors could take an elevator to the tower observation deck for breathtaking views and a complimentary stick of Wrigley chewing gum.

Tribune Tower

John Mead Howells and Raymond Hood,
1925

In 1922 the Tribune Company's
owners announced a competition
with a $50,000 prize. The quest? To design "the most beautiful and distinctive office building
in the world." The winning entry was a tower with chamfered corners and recessed vertical
ribbon windows. The Gothic crown and flying buttresses lent the building an air both imposing
and refined.

The Tribune Tower's most popular feature is its base, where 150 stone fragments are
embedded in the exterior wall. At the request of Colonel Robert McCormick, the power-
ful head of the *Tribune,* journalists gathered fragments of historically significant buildings from
around the world. The pieces came from sites and structures such as the Taj Mahal in India, the
Great Wall of China, and the Alamo in Texas.

In 1881 a grocery store occupied the southwest corner of Michigan Avenue and Wacker Drive. Its owner erected a sign that honored the site of old Fort Dearborn.

360 North Michigan

(right) Alfred S. Alschuler, 1923
Lohan Associates, restoration, 2001

Alfred Alschuler designed 360 North Michigan to fit its polygonal lot. Its upper floors are twelve-sided. The building's Beaux-Arts design features Corinthian columns that flank the central arch and allegorical figures that depict Chicago's early history. The top three stories form a classical colonnade, which is topped by a small Greco-Roman temple. The building's original owner, shipping insurer London Guarantee and Accident Company, placed its headquarters near the busiest port in the world.

333 North Michigan

(left) Holabird & Root, 1928

The art deco details, setbacks, and strong vertical lines of 333 North Michigan display the influence of Eliel Saarinen's second-place Tribune Tower competition entry. Its base is polished black and purple marble, and the rest of the building is clad in light limestone and sculpted terra cotta. The reliefs by Fred Torrey depict Native Americans, early traders, Marquette and Jolliet, and Chicago's settlers.

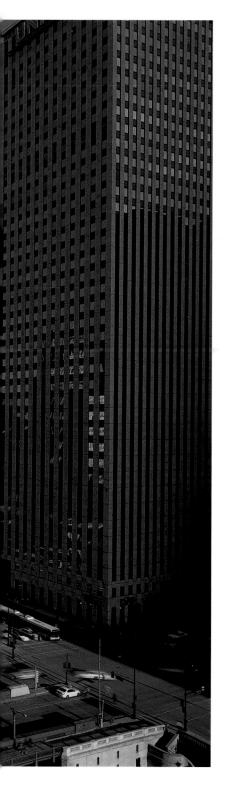

Wacker Drive, 1929

75 East Wacker

(tower, left) Herbert Hugh Riddle, 1928

Cattle-car magnate Alonzo C. Mather commissioned Herbert Hugh Riddle to design an impressive skyscraper. Working within Chicago's 1923 zoning ordinance, Riddle pushed the building to its allowable height of 264 feet and added a narrow tower. Towers were allowed under the zoning ordinance if they were unoccupied and took up no more than one-fourth of the building's footprint. Because the lot was just 65 feet wide and 100 feet deep, 75 East Wacker was Chicago's most slender skyscraper.

35 East Wacker

(right, with dome) Giaver & Dinkelberg; Thielbar & Fugard, 1926

Originally called the Jeweler's Building, 35 East Wacker contained a wholesale jewelry market. To protect merchandise, buyers and sellers drove their cars into a basement elevator and were transported to their desired floor. This was not the most practical amenity, as car elevators required more maintenance than passenger elevators and eliminated valuable floor space. The elevator was dismantled after just fourteen years of service. The building's dome was once the Stratosphere Lounge, a legendary speakeasy that was rumored to be a favorite hangout of Al Capone. Today it houses the presentation gallery for the architectural firm of Helmut Jahn.

Trump Tower Chicago

Skidmore, Owings & Merrill, 2009

The 92-story Trump Tower was designed to complement its setting. Each of its setbacks will relate to a nearby building. The first honors the top of the Wrigley Building; the second aligns with the roof of Marina City; and the third setback is at the height of 330 North Wabash. The Trump Tower's curved shape and silvery-blue stainless steel, aluminum, and glass curtain are intended to reflect the river's color and curvature. The design contrasts, however, with the Beaux-Arts elegance of the Wrigley Building and the stark modernism of Ludwig Mies van der Rohe's 330 North Wabash.

330 North Wabash

Office of Mies van der Rohe; C. F. Murphy Associates, 1973

Once known as the IBM Building, 330 North Wabash was Ludwig Mies van der Rohe's last skyscraper in America. Its design embodies his architectural tenet of simplicity. Because of the building's proximity to the river and its location on the bend, the dark bronze facade seems to rise from the green water.

321 North Clark

(left) Skidmore, Owings & Merrill, 1987

The modernist design of the 321 North Clark pays homage to the functional, austere architecture of Ludwig Mies van der Rohe. What sets this tower apart from many Miesian buildings is its relationship to the river. Instead of turning its back on the waterway, the lobby seems to flow out to the river's edge.

Marina City

(far right) Bertrand Goldberg, 1964

Marina City embodies Bertrand Goldberg's vision for the modern American metropolis. Believing that urban areas should be centers of "synergy, growth, and community," he faced two major challenges: the flight of the middle class to the suburbs and zoning ordinances that restricted mixed-use development. His eye was on the future, and with funding from the union of building janitors and elevator operators—who had an interest in urban growth—he convinced officials to ease zoning and laid out a city-within-a-city. When completed, Marina City consisted of two residential towers, an office building, a bowling alley, swimming pool, health club, restaurant, and stores.

Reid Murdoch Building

George C. Nimmons, 1914

This building helps one imagine what a stroll along the banks of the Chicago River would have been like near the beginning of the twentieth century. Architect George Nimmons combined characteristics of Chicago industrial architecture and the Prairie School to build an attractive and practical grocer's warehouse. The building's clock tower was a public amenity that hid a large water tank. Around 1926 the warehouse underwent some changes to accommodate the widening of LaSalle Drive. A flat roof replaced the original, which had low-pitched gables, and the westernmost bay was removed.

Leo Burnett Building

(left) Kevin Roche/John Dinkeloo & Associates; Shaw & Associates, 1989

In keeping with postmodernism, which exploits traditional architectural conventions, the Burnett Building revives Chicago's turn-of-the-century commercial style. The structure features a tripartite facade, divided like a classical column's base, shaft, and capital. Whereas many modernist buildings boldly display their steel, this structure is clad in granite. The colonnade at the base is repeated on a smaller scale at the fifteenth floor, acknowledging its neighbor, 55 West Wacker.

United Airlines Building

(right) DeStefano & Partners; Ricardo Bofill Arquitectura, 1992

The designers of the United Airlines Building, at 77 West Wacker Drive, took as their inspiration the classical column, a popular feature in buildings from the 1880s to early 1900s. The components of a classical column helped architects devise an aesthetic solution to high-rise architecture. Designing a building so that it resembled a column stressed verticality and provided a unified appearance. The "base" of 77 West Wacker is sheathed in white granite; the "shaft" draws the eye skyward with long vertical pilasters; and the "capital" features arched windows and a pediment reminiscent of ancient Greek temples.

LaSalle-Wacker Building

(left) Holabird & Root; Rebori, Wentworth, Dewey & McCormick, 1930

The art deco LaSalle-Wacker Building was built in the form of an H, which optimized access to light and air while maximizing floor space. Chicago's 1923 zoning ordinance required setbacks when buildings reached 264 feet. The north light court (the inner part of the H) is visible in the photograph. At the twenty-third story, a tower rises another eighteen floors.

222 North LaSalle

(right) Graham, Anderson, Probst & White, 1927
Skidmore, Owings & Merrill, addition, 1986

This structure, originally called the Builders Building, was intended as a showplace for the construction industry. The atrium served as an indoor exhibition space for product displays. When Skidmore, Owings & Merrill designed the western addition, they maintained the building's original proportions and composition. The four-story glass-sheathed penthouse that connects the two sides is a modernist touch.

325 North Wells

L. Gustav Hallberg, 1912; Booth Hansen, renovation, 1984

Originally a warehouse, 325 North Wells is an excellent example of Chicago's early commercial architecture. Undecorated masonry piers and spandrels enclose the steel frame that lies beneath. A glass addition at the top reinterprets the building's original cornice and houses a boardroom, conference facilities, and executive offices. The green-tinted glass contrasts with the red brick and complements the river's hue.

Merchandise Mart

Graham, Anderson, Probst & White, 1930

Marshall Field and Company built the Merchandise Mart to centralize and modernize its wholesale merchandising, which was scattered in at least thirteen different Chicago warehouses. The enormous facility, over four million square feet of space, was the largest commercial building of its day. The Great Depression, however, forced Field's out of the wholesale market, and the $32 million investment stood half empty until it was purchased by Joseph P. Kennedy in 1945 for one-half of its original cost.

The Mart's limestone streamlined art deco facade features recessed vertical bands of windows, counterpoints to the building's horizontal mass. The entry lobby features murals by Jules Guerin, the illustrator of Burnham's *Plan of Chicago*. In 1953 Kennedy created the Merchant's Hall of Fame along the river esplanade "to immortalize outstanding American merchants." These bronze busts include Marshall Field, Edward Albert Filene, George Huntington Hartford, Julius Rosenwald, John Wanamaker, Aaron Montgomery Ward, Franklin Winfield Woolworth, and Robert Elkington Wood.

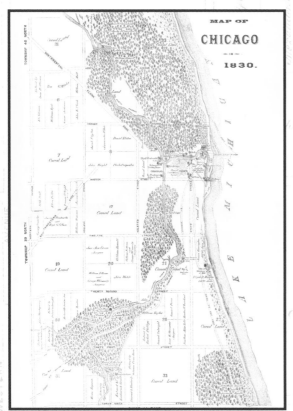

Erie on the Park, *Lucien Lagrange & Associates, 2002*

Chicago's waterways, 1830

THE NORTH BRANCH

In Lake County, just north of Chicago, three forks meet to form the North Branch of the Chicago River. A mixed landscape of marshes and woods, the North Branch was much used in the 1830s for recreational activities such as swimming, ice skating, and fishing.

While the North Branch did not play as much of a role in the industrial and commercial growth of Chicago as the South Branch or the Main Branch, early settlers deforested, drained, and ditched the adjacent lands to exploit the rich soil. A layer of ceramic tiles laid underground prevented fields from soaking up excess water, which ditches diverted to the river. Erosion and deforestation contributed to floods all along the North Branch; they frequently reached the downtown area.

The many recent building conversion projects and residential developments demonstrate that the North Branch has become a desirable place to live. But a boat trip up the river still reveals a quiet, forestlike setting only a few miles from the metropolis.

The North Branch, c. 1902

WOLF POINT—
Where the Branches Meet

Wolf Point marks the location where the three branches of the Chicago River meet. It was the site of some of Chicago's earliest buildings. According to A. T. Andreas's *History of Chicago* (1884), James Kinzie and Archibald Caldwell built the town's first tavern on the west side of the river in 1829—the building at far left in the drawing. After killing one of the wolves that reportedly terrorized the area, the tavern's second owner hung out a sign depicting the beast, thereby giving his business—and the place—its name. But Juliette Kinzie, one of Chicago's earliest settlers (her husband was James Kinzie's half brother), wrote that the area was called Wolf Point because it had been the residence of an Indian named Moaway, meaning "the Wolf."

Wolf Point represents a balance between the natural and built environments. Native trees and plants offer animal habitats. Riverwalk visitors might glimpse one of more than seventy species of fish or a peregrine falcon. The beavers are so prolific that fences were installed to protect the trees.

Wolf Point, 1833

Residences at Riverbend

(left) DeStefano & Partners, 2002

The facade of Residences at Riverbend curves with the river's graceful arc. Working with a shallow lot, architect Robert Bistry eliminated the standard central hallway. Instead the corridors run along the west side of the building, and all units have a river view. The lowest levels are townhouses; above them is a garage. Elevators lift cars into the garage because the building is too narrow for a ramp.

Fulton House

(right) Frank Abbott, 1908
Harry Weese & Associates, renovation, 1981

Fulton House was originally the American Cold Storage Warehouse, and its repurposing as a residential structure brought surprising challenges. To keep stored products cool, the concrete floors were up to two feet thick, the outer walls were four feet thick, and there were no windows. Rooms were lined with horsehair or cork and cooled by a combination of brine and ammonia that flowed through two-inch steel pipes set along the floors and walls.

In 1979 architect Harry Weese converted the building to loft-style condominiums. It took eighteen months to defrost the structure and required about 500 semi trucks to haul away the insulation. Holes were punched through the walls to create windows and balconies. Weese, who had a love for water and sailing, included docks for residents with boats.

Chicago's first railroad depot, Canal and Kinzie Streets, c. 1850

River Cottages

Harry Weese & Associates, 1990

Illinois native Harry Weese rejected "square box" modernism, believing that only after seeing everything ever built could an architect establish a doctrine. Though he did not quite see everything, Weese's work does reflect his travels, experiences, and especially his nautical bent. His River Cottages were a culmination of his enthusiasm for boating and his desire to see the Chicago River cleaned and revitalized. On the site of Chicago's earliest railroad depot, Weese designed four townhouses that celebrate their riverside location. Their triangular accents represent ship sails; the round windows resemble portholes; and each unit has a private dock.

East Bank Club

Ezra Gordon—Jack M. Levin Associates, 1979

Compared to the River Cottages across the waterway, the East Bank Club is a reminder
of widespread perceptions of the polluted and neglected river in the 1970s. The massive,
unadorned concrete structure turns its back on the water. Today it is unlikely that a prestigious
sports center and private health club would shut out a view of the Chicago River.

Kinzie Park

Pappageorge/Haymes, mid-rise units and townhouses, 2000
Nagle Hartray Danker Kagan McKay Penney Architects, high rise (not pictured), 2002

If the East Bank Club snubs the river, and the River Cottages mark an early desire for river residence, Kinzie Park exemplifies a revived enthusiasm for the river as a valuable natural asset and property enhancer. This gated community was built just after the city mandated that new construction had to allow access to the Riverwalk. If a nonresident pedestrian wants to enter the site, he must notify the attendant.

River Bank Lofts

Nimmons & Fellows, 1909

George Nimmons, who also designed the Reid Murdoch Building on the Main Branch, was one of the country's most sought-after industrial architects. This was due, in part, to the commission he won to design the Sears, Roebuck and Company's complex in downtown Chicago. He was also known for decorative details such as the horizontal courses and the terra-cotta corner accents still visible on the converted River Bank Lofts. These gave the utilitarian buildings distinct identities. Today River Bank Lofts is an excellent example of the numerous conversions of early-twentieth-century warehouses and industrial buildings taking place along the North Branch.

Erie on the Park

Lucien Lagrange & Associates, 2002

Lucien Lagrange's Erie on the Park displays a conscious approach to location. The lot's irregular footprint determined the building's trapezoidal shape, which increases access to natural light and air. Triangular vertical trusses run up the building for wind bracing, reminiscent of a skyscraper that Lagrange worked on while at Skidmore, Owings & Merrill: the John Hancock Center.

Montgomery Ward Complex

Schmidt, Garden & Martin, original warehouse and office building (left), 1908
Willis J. McCauley, second warehouse (right), 1930
Minoru Yamasaki & Associates, corporate offices (high rise, center), 1972
Lohan Associates; Pappageorge/Haymes, renovation, 2004

Montgomery Ward was a successful Chicago-based mail-order business at the turn of the century. The company needed an enormous space to fill all types of orders—from clothes to dishes to prefabricated homes. The original warehouse, called the Montgomery Ward & Co. Catalog House, curved low along the river, its red brick spandrels emphasizing its horizontality. The design of the second warehouse highlighted verticality. Ward's 1972 corporate high rise was a deliberate departure from the rest of the buildings, a looming monolith that juts above its industrial predecessors. The entire complex was recently converted to condominiums.

The South Branch and Wacker Drive

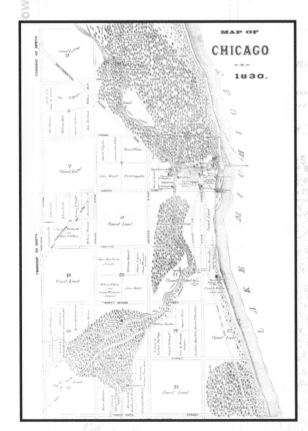

Chicago's waterways, 1830

THE SOUTH BRANCH

The South Branch was once a clean creek alive with plants and animals. It originated at Mud Lake, which connected the Chicago and Des Plaines rivers during the wet season. To connect the two rivers permanently, engineers built the Illinois and Michigan Canal between 1836 and 1848.

In the late nineteenth century, Chicago became the meatpacking capital of the country as trains delivered livestock to the Union Stock Yards on Chicago's South Side for sale, sorting, and slaughter. Because antipollution ordinances were irregularly enforced, a great deal of animal waste was dumped into the South Fork of the South Branch, which became known as Bubbly Creek. Here is the testimony of Ed Lace, a Chicagoan who grew up nearby:

> As the offal [animal carcasses] settled to the bottom it began to rot. Grease separated and rose to the surface. Bubbles of methane formed on the bed of the river and rose to the surface, which was coated with grease. Some of these bubbles were quite large and when they burst, a stink arose. There were many local names for this part of the river, most unprintable.

With the construction of the Sanitary and Ship Canal and the decline of the stockyards, the South Branch began to flush itself and the South Fork was filled in. Today the downtown portion of the South Branch is home to some of the city's most prestigious companies, and its banks are lined with architecture that emphasizes Chicago's business and financial might.

Bubbly Creek, c. 1905

WATER STREET BECOMES WACKER DRIVE

As part of an ambitious plan to transform Chicago, in 1909 planners Daniel Burnham and Edward H. Bennett proposed to ease congestion on Water Street by moving commercial traffic to a second level below grade. Their hope was to spur the growth of impressive and beautiful architecture along the river. The street was renamed Wacker Drive for Charles H. Wacker, the chairman of the Chicago Plan Commission, who championed the roadway.

In 1998 Mayor Richard M. Daley supported the Riverwalk master plan, which would revitalize Wacker Drive by adding paved riverside pathways, bike paths to the suburbs, access to the river, docks for boaters, scenic overlooks, fishing centers, and new parks.

225 West Wacker

(left) Kohn Pedersen Fox; Perkins & Will, 1989

Kohn Pedersen Fox's postmodern design for 225 West Wacker reinterprets the classical column. Its tripartite form features a two-story base, a central shaft, and a capital with four futuristic towers. Its gray granite sheathing contrasts with its neighbor to the west at 333 and celebrates the river with round porthole windows and an integrated "bridge" at the top of the structure.

333 West Wacker

(center) Kohn Pedersen Fox; Perkins & Will, 1983

The design of 333 West Wacker had a major impact on the river architecture of Chicago. The architects' appreciation of and consideration for the setting distinguished their building from the many glass-and-steel boxes erected along the river in the previous two decades. Kohn Pedersen Fox's work challenged other architects to respect the river. Instead of conforming to its lot, the curve of the facade complements the bend in the river. The tinted glass harmonizes with the water and changes with the sky. On the sides that face away from the river, porthole windows line the base, and decorative details reflect the city grid.

Great Lakes Building

(foreground, low) Holabird & Roche, original building, 1912

George Schipporeit, renovation, 1983

191 North Wacker

(right) Kohn Pedersen Fox; Perkins & Will, 2002

These two buildings present a contrast in style, recalling the historically diverse perspectives on the role of the river in Chicago architecture. The Great Lakes Building, at 180 North Wacker, is typical of Holabird & Roche's approach to clear proportion and design; one thinks of the warehouses and industrial buildings that turned their back on the river. In comparison, 191 North Wacker pays homage to its location by reflecting its surroundings in blue tinted glass.

100 North Riverside

Perkins & Will, 1990

When Perkins & Will designed 100 North Riverside, they met with Amtrak to discuss how to position support caissons within the network of railroad tracks below the site. But the architects discovered that the track configuration would not allow for caissons under the building's southwest corner. So they designed a truss system that relies on the southeast corner as a support for a cantilever.

Civic Opera Building

Graham, Anderson, Probst & White, 1929

When utilities tycoon Samuel Insull, the "Prince of Electricity," commissioned a new opera building for Chicago, he wanted a facility that would bring music to the masses. The result was a design in the art deco armchair form, giving the building its nickname of "Insull's Throne." The entrance along Wacker Drive features musical instrument reliefs, a two-story portico, and a grand pedestrian walkway. To provide additional income and keep shows affordable, most of the building is multiuse rental space. The Lyric Opera Building (as it was originally called) opened to the public with *Aïda* just six days after the market crash that launched the Great Depression.

Chicago Daily News Building concept drawing, 1929

Riverside Plaza

Holabird & Root, 1929

Holabird & Root's design for the Chicago Daily News Building reinforced the newspaper's power and prestige. Vertical bands of windows reach skyward and balance the building's massive multitiered base. The shallow sculptural reliefs on the lower wings honor journalism and Pulitzer Prize winners. Constructed over subterranean railroad tracks, the building stands on a network of columns. A complex air-handling system redirects exhaust from the diesel trains below.

Chicago Mercantile Exchange Center

Fujikawa, Johnson & Associates, 1983, 1987

The Chicago Mercantile Exchange Center, often referred to as the Merc, consists of two 40-story office towers connected by an 11-story pavilion that houses two stacked trading floors. The towers' serrated corners mean sixteen corner offices per floor. The original exchange was at the northwest corner of Franklin and Washington streets, just one block away. The exchange evolved from the Chicago Butter and Egg Board, which was established in 1898 to trade those two products. Today it is the CME Group, a merger of the Mercantile Exchange and the Chicago Board of Trade. Exchange traders primarily buy and sell futures contracts on interest rates, equity indexes, and foreign exchange.

200 South Wacker

Harry Weese & Associates, 1981

The trapezoidal shape of 200 South Wacker creates dramatic angles, as do many of Harry Weese's other buildings, including the River Cottages and the Swissôtel. The building is made up of adjoining triangular towers. The exterior columns are set on an angle to optimize river views. The three-story, glass-enclosed lobby is set back from the perimeter, creating a pedestrian arcade along the water's edge.

Sears Tower

(left) Skidmore, Owings & Merrill, 1973, 1985
DeStefano & Partners, 1993

The distinctive silhouette of the Sears Tower is a result of its structural system. Fazlur Khan, the building's structural engineer, designed nine bundled tubes, each 75 feet square in plan. Two tubes stop at the fifty-fifth floor; two end at the sixty-sixth floor; three stop at the ninetieth floor; and the remaining two rise to the top. These terminal points balance aesthetics with the lateral stiffness needed for wind bracing and height. At 110 stories, the Sears Tower is the most notable feature of the Chicago skyline—it was the world's tallest building until 1998.

311 South Wacker Drive

(right) Kohn Pedersen Fox; HKS, 1990

When the castlelike 311 South Wacker was completed, it drew unexpected attention. At night, two thousand fluorescent tubes lit up the building's glass crown. The lights were so bright they interfered with birds' migratory patterns. In time they were dimmed to reduce avian disorientation.

Gateway Center IV

Skidmore, Owings & Merrill, 1983

The Gateway Center buildings reveal Skidmore, Owings & Merrill's transition from modernist design to a postmodernism that relates to its setting. While Gateway Centers I, II (renamed CDW Plaza), and III are typical Miesian office buildings, Gateway IV acknowledges its riverside location with green glass and a curved facade.

© Anthony May Photography

Thermal Chicago Corporation

Franklin/Van Buren
District Cooling Plant

Eckenhoff Saunders Architects, 1996

The Thermal Chicago cooling plant furthers the city's ambition to become the greenest city in the world. Designed for a utilitarian purpose, the building's green glass facade captures the beauty of its river location. One of five currently operating in the city, the cooling plant is a large slush maker. Overnight, when electricity rates are lowest, it chills water to just below 32 degrees Fahrenheit with help from glycol, a coolant. The slush is pumped through insulated underground pipes to nearby office buildings to provide cooling. The liquid then returns to the plant, and the process is repeated. When electricity rates rise during the day, the plant cuts production. The process is pollutant-free and uses no chlorofluorocarbons.

Old Chicago Main Post Office

Graham, Anderson, Probst & White, 1921, 1932

In the early twentieth century, Chicago required a central mail-sorting facility to accommodate large mail-order companies and the Federal Reserve, which printed notes and stock certificates in vast numbers. The old post office's massive structure is anchored by four corner towers, and its appearance is lightened by uninterrupted vertical windows. Today the facility sits empty, waiting for a redevelopment plan.

New Chicago Main Post Office

Knight Architects Engineers Planners, 1996

Chicago's new main post office is the largest and most complex in the nation, consisting of three interlocking pavilions for mail processing, administration, and public service. The federal government owns the property and was not required to provide Riverwalk access—though there is a landscaped green space at the river's edge.

River City

Bertrand Goldberg, 1986

A critic of decentralization and suburbanization, and a strong believer in cities, Bertrand Goldberg designed River City as an urban community for living, working, and playing. The complex is two intertwined S-shaped concrete buildings joined by an atrium. "River Road" runs through the center of the atrium and is designed to resemble a quaint European street with benches, streetlights, and trees. Goldberg envisioned a miniature city that would provide all of life's necessities through shops, offices, childcare centers, and other facilities. Chicago's planning commission would not grant the necessary mixed-use permits, however, for fear that the area would be too densely developed. Goldberg was able to incorporate some of the city-within-a-city elements: marina, apothecary, and grocery store.

INDEX OF ARCHITECTS

INDEX OF BUILDINGS

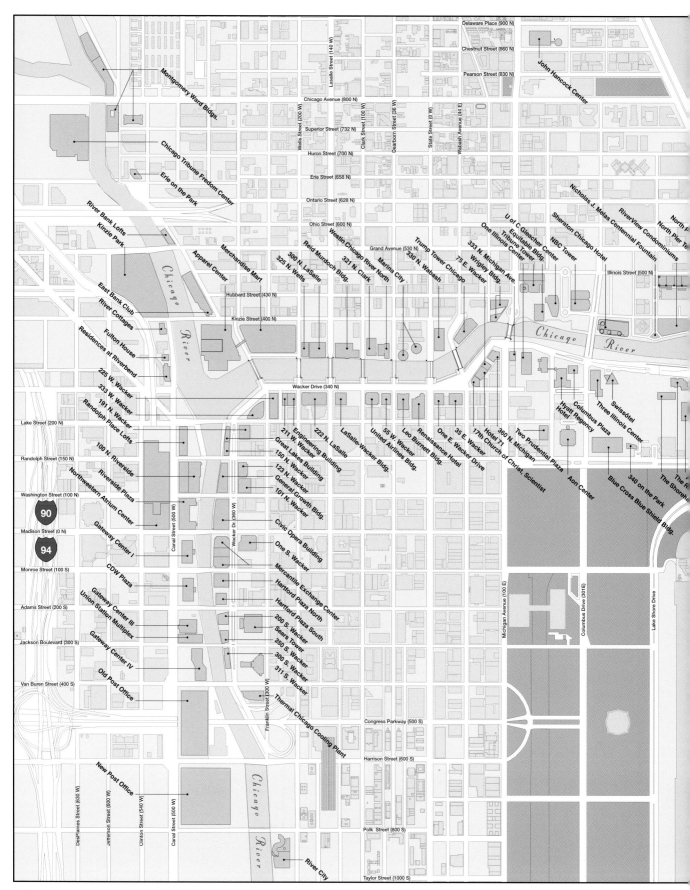

Delaware Place (900 N)

Chestnut Street (860 N)

Pearson Street (830 N)

John Hancock Center

LaSalle Street (140 W)

Chicago Avenue (800 N)

Wells Street (200 W)

Clark Street (100 W)

Dearborn Street (36 W)

State Street (0 W)

Wabash Avenue (44 E)

Montgomery Ward Bldgs.

Superior Street (732 N)

Huron Street (700 N)

Chicago Tribune Fredom Center

Erie Street (658 N)

Erie on the Park

Ontario Street (628 N)

River Bank Lofts

Kinzie Park

Ohio Street (600 N)

Grand Avenue (530 N)

Nicholas J. Melas Centennial Fountain

RiverView Condominiums

North P

North Pier Te

Westin Chicago River North

Trump Tower Chicago

U of C Gleacher Center

Sheraton Chicago Hotel

Apparel Center

Merchandise Mart

300 N. LaSalle

325 N. Wells

Reid Murdoch Bldg.

321 N. Clark

Marina City

330 N. Wabash

333 N. Michigan Ave.

75 E. Wacker

Equitable Bldg.

One Illinois Center

Tribune Tower

Wrigley Bldg.

NBC Tower

Illinois Street (500 N)

East Bank Club

River Cottages

Hubbard Street (430 N)

Kinzie Street (400 N)

Chicago River

Fulton House

Residences at Riverbend

225 W. Wacker

333 W. Wacker

191 N. Wacker

Randolph Place Lofts

Wacker Drive (340 N)

Columbus Plaza

Hyatt Regency Hotel

Three Illinois Center

Swissôtel

Lake Street (200 N)

100 N. Riverside

Engineering Building

222 N. LaSalle

LaSalle-Wacker Bldg.

United Airlines Bldg.

55 W. Wacker

Leo Burnett Bldg.

Renaissance Hotel

One E. Wacker

35 E. Wacker

17th Church of Christ, Scientist

Hotel 71

360 N. Michigan

Two Prudential Plaza

Aon Center

340 on the Park

Blue Cross Blue Shield Bldg.

The Sh

The R

The Shoreh

Randolph Street (150 N)

Riverside Plaza

211 W. Wacker

Great Lakes Building

150 N. Wacker

123 N. Wacker

General Growth Bldg.

101 N. Wacker

Northwestern Atrium Center

Washington Street (100 N)

90

Madison Street (0 N)

94

Canal Street (500 W)

Wacker Dr. (360 W)

Civic Opera Building

Gateway Center I

Monroe Street (100 S)

CDW Plaza

One S. Wacker

Mercantile Exchange Center

Hartford Plaza North

Michigan Avenue (100 E)

Columbus Drive (301 E)

Lake Shore Drive

Gateway Center III

Union Station Multiplex

Adams Street (200 S)

Hartford Plaza South

200 S. Wacker

Sears Tower

Gateway Center IV

Jackson Boulevard (300 S)

250 S. Wacker

300 S. Wacker

311 S. Wacker

Old Post Office

Van Buren Street (400 S)

DesPlaines Street (630 W)

Jefferson Street (600 W)

Clinton Street (540 W)

Canal Street (500 W)

Franklin Street (300 W)

Thermal Chicago Cooling Plant

Congress Parkway (500 S)

New Post Office

Harrison Street (600 S)

Chicago River

Polk Street (800 S)

River City

Taylor Street (1000 S)

SPOTTING MAP

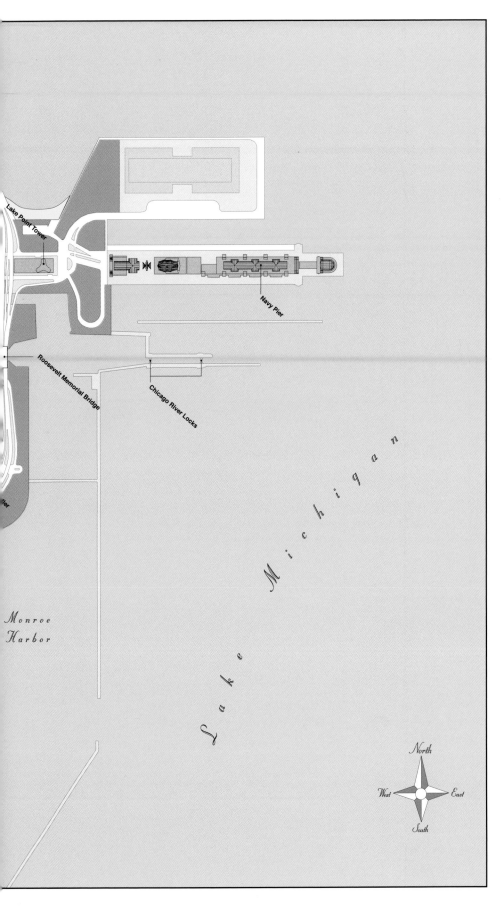

Lake Point Tower

Navy Pier

Roosevelt Memorial Bridge

Chicago River Locks

Monroe Harbor

Lake Michigan

North

West

East

South

THANKS

the Chicago Architecture Foundation is indebted to the staff members who helped create this publication: Sarah Arehart, Anne Evans, Barbara Gordon, Jean Linsner, Jennifer Masengarb, and Billy Shelton. We also acknowledge the staff at Chicago's First Lady cruises.

Jennifer thanks Marcus for his understanding and Mattison for agreeing with her mom that Chicago is the best city in the world.

IMAGE CREDITS